NO

NOW ZEN

Charlotte Joko Beck

Edited by Steve Smith

HarperSanFrancisco
A Division of HarperCollins*Publishers*

Harper San Francisco and the author, in association with the Basic Founda-
tion, a not-for-profit organization whose primary mission is reforestation, will
facilitate the planting of two trees for every one tree used in the manufacture
of this book.

The essays in this work were originally published in *Everyday Zen* (Harper
San Francisco, 1989) and *Nothing Special* (Harper San Francisco, 1993), by
Charlotte Joko Beck with Steve Smith.

"Beginning Zen Practice" and "Practicing with Relationships" are re-
vised versions of talks copyrighted by the Zen Center of Los Angeles, and
are reprinted with the permission of ZCLA.

NOW ZEN. Copyright © 1995 by Charlotte Joko Beck. All rights reserved.
Printed in the United States of America. No part of this book may be used or
reproduced in any manner whatsoever without written permission except in
the case of brief quotations embodied in critical articles and reviews. For in-
formation address HarperCollins Publishers, 10 East 53rd Street, New York,
NY 10022.

FIRST EDITION

Library of Congress Cataloging-in-Publication Data:
Beck, Charlotte Joko.
Now Zen / Charlotte Joko Beck ; edited by Steve Smith.
p. cm.
ISBN 0-06-251173-4
1. Religious life—Zen Buddhism. I. Smith, Steve. II. Title.
BQ9286.2.B444   1995
294.3'444—dc20

94-28126
CIP

95 96 97 98 99 ❖ HAD 10 9 8 7 6 5 4 3 2

This edition is printed on acid-free paper that meets the American National
Standards Institute Z39.48 Standard.

CONTENTS

PREFACE

From the heart of Charlotte Joko Beck's teachings, the simplicity of Zen shines forth: plain, transparent, cleansed of unnecessary paradox and obfuscation. Joko shows that spiritual practice means working with our life as it is—our loves and losses, relationships and yearnings, work and leisure. Her keen intelligence and disarming directness cut through illusion to reality itself. In the mirror of her words we see ourselves more clearly, and gain courage to face what is true.

Zen practice is awakening fully to our lives, here and now. In organic growth—from root through stem to flower—we uncover that which is hidden, enlarge our embrace, and come to rest in this moment. Joko's life experiences as musician, mother, secretary, administrator, and finally teacher to countless Zen students over the years equip her superbly to assist us along our unique paths.

Wisdom is truth that nourishes. The words comprising this book are no more than fingers pointing at the moon: they will find their true justification in more successful lives of compassion, service, and joy.

Steve Smith

Claremont, California
March 1994

NOW ZEN

ONE

ROOT

BEGINNING ZEN PRACTICE

My dog doesn't worry about the meaning of life. She may worry if she doesn't get her breakfast, but she doesn't sit around worrying about whether she will get fulfilled or liberated or enlightened. As long as she gets some food and a little affection, her life is fine. But we human beings are not like dogs. We have self-centered minds which get us into plenty of trouble. If we do not come to understand the error in the way we think, our self-awareness, which is our greatest blessing, is also our downfall.

To some degree we all find life difficult, perplexing, and oppressive. Even when it goes well, as it may for a time, we worry that it probably won't keep on that way. Depending on our personal history, we arrive at adulthood with very mixed feelings about this life. If I were to tell you that your life is already perfect, whole, and complete just as it is, you would think I was crazy. Nobody believes his or her life is perfect. And yet there is something within each of us that basically knows we are boundless, limitless. We are caught in the contradiction of finding life a rather perplexing puzzle which causes us a lot of misery, and at the same time being dimly aware of the boundless, limitless nature of life. So we begin looking for an answer to the puzzle.

The first way of looking is to seek a solution outside ourselves. At first this may be on a very ordinary level. There are many people in the world who feel that if only they had a bigger car, a nicer house, better vacations, a more understanding boss, or a more interesting partner, then their life would work. We all go through that one. Slowly we wear out most of our "if onlies." "If only I had this, or that, then my life would work." Not one of us isn't, to some degree, still wearing out our "if onlies." First of all we wear out those on the gross levels. Then we shift our search to more subtle levels. Finally, in looking for the thing outside of ourselves that we hope is going to complete us, we turn to a spiritual discipline. Unfortunately we tend to bring into this new search the same orientation as before. Most people who come to the Zen Center don't think a Cadillac will do it, but they think that enlightenment will. Now they've got a new cookie, a new "if only." "If only I could understand what realization is all about, I would be happy." "If only I could have at least a little enlightenment experience, I would be happy." Coming into a practice like Zen, we bring our usual notions that we are going to get somewhere— become enlightened—and get all the cookies that have eluded us in the past.

Our whole life consists of this little subject looking outside itself for an object. But if you take something that is limited, like body and mind, and look for something outside it, that something becomes an object and must be limited too. So you have something limited looking for something limited and you just end up with more of the same folly that has made you miserable.

We have all spent many years building up a conditioned view of life. There is "me" and there is this "thing" out there that is either hurting me or pleasing me. We tend to run our whole life trying to avoid all that hurts or displeases us, noticing the objects, people, or situations that we think will give us pain or pleasure, avoiding one and pursuing the other. Without exception, we all do this. We remain separate from our life, looking at it, analyzing it, judging it, seeking to answer the questions, "What am I going to get out of it? Is it going to give me pleasure or comfort or should I run away from it?" We do this from morning until night. Underneath our nice, friendly facades there is great unease. If I were to scratch below the surface of anyone I would find fear, pain, and anxiety running amok. We all have ways to cover them up. We overeat, overdrink, overwork; we watch too much television. We are always doing something to cover up our basic existential anxiety. Some people live that way until the day they die. As the years go by, it gets worse and worse. What might not look so bad when you are twenty-five looks awful by the time you are fifty. We all know people who might as well be dead; they have so contracted into their limited viewpoints that it is as painful for those around them as it is for themselves. The flexibility and joy and flow of life are gone. And that rather grim possibility faces all of us, unless we wake up to the fact that we need to work with our life, we need to practice. We have to see through the mirage that there is an "I" separate from "that." Our practice is to close the gap. Only in that instant when we and the object become one can we see what our life is.

Enlightenment is not something you achieve. It is the absence of something. All your life you have been going forward after something, pursuing some goal.

Enlightenment is dropping all that. But to talk about it is of little use. The practice has to be done by each individual. There is no substitute. We can read about it until we are a thousand years old and it won't do a thing for us. We all have to practice, and we have to practice with all of our might for the rest of our lives.

What we really want is a natural life. Our lives are so unnatural that to do a practice like Zen is, in the beginning, extremely difficult. But once we begin to get a glimmer that the problem in life is not outside ourselves, we have begun to walk down this path. Once that awakening starts, once we begin to see that life can be more open and joyful than we had ever thought possible, we want to practice.

We enter a discipline like Zen practice so that we can learn to live in a sane way. Zen is almost a thousand years old and the kinks have been worked out of it; while it is not easy, it is not insane. It is down to earth and very practical. It is about our daily life. It is about working better in the office, raising our kids better, and having better relationships. Having a more sane and satisfying life must come out of a sane, balanced practice. What we want to do is to find some way of working with the basic insanity that exists because of our blindness.

It takes courage to sit well. Zen is not a discipline for everyone. We have to be willing to do something that is not easy. If we do it with patience and perseverance, with the guidance of a good teacher, then gradually our life settles down, becomes more balanced. Our emotions are not quite as domineering. As we sit, we find that the primary thing we must work with is our busy, chaotic mind. We are all caught up in frantic thinking, and the problem in practice is to begin to bring that thinking into clarity and balance. When the mind becomes clear and balanced and is no longer caught by objects, there can be an opening—and for a second we can realize who we really are.

But sitting is not something that we do for a year or two with the idea of mastering it. Sitting is something we do for a lifetime. There is no end to the opening up that is possible for a human being. Eventually we see that we are the limitless, boundless ground of the universe. Our job for the rest of our life is to open up into that immensity and to express it. Having more and more contact with this reality always brings compassion for others and changes our daily life. We live differently, work differently, relate to people differently. Zen is a lifelong study. It isn't just sitting on a cushion for thirty or forty minutes a day. Our whole life becomes practice, twenty-four hours a day.

PRISONERS OF FEAR

We all know the picture of the important executive working until ten o'clock at night, answering the phone, grabbing a sandwich on the run. His poor body is being short-changed. He thinks his frantic efforts are essential for "the good life"; he fails to see that desire is running his life—and it runs all of ours, too. Because we are controlled by our desires, we have only a dim awareness of the basic truth of our existence.

Most people who don't do any kind of practice are pretty selfish. They are caught up in desires: to be important, to possess this or that, to be rich, famous. Of course that's true of all of us, to a degree. But as we practice we begin to suspect that our life is not working quite the way the TV commercials say it will. Television advertisements suggest that if you have the newest hair spray and makeup and garage door opener, you life is going to be great. Right? Well, most of us find that isn't true. And as we see that, we begin to see that the way we live isn't working. The selfish greed which runs our lives is not working.

Then we begin a second stage: "Well, if it doesn't work to be selfish, then I'm going to be unselfish." Most religious practices (and some Zen practices, I'm sorry to say) are about unselfishness. Seeing our meanness, our unkindness, we decide to pursue a new desire: to be kind, to be good, to be patient. Guilt goes with this desire, like a sort of baby brother: when we don't fulfill our picture of how we should be, we feel guilty. We're still trying to be something we're not. We're trying to figure out how to be different than we are. When we can't fulfill our ideals, we build guilt and depression. In our practice we swing through both of these stages. We see that we are mean, greedy, violent, selfish, ambitious. And so we form a new ambition, to be unselfish. "I shouldn't have those thoughts. I've been sitting for such a long time; why am I still greedy and mean? I should be better than that by now." We're all doing that. A lot of religious practice mistakenly aims at trying to produce a good person who doesn't do or think bad things. Some Zen centers are caught up in this approach, too. It leads to a kind of arrogance and self-righteousness because if you are doing it *right,* what about all the others who don't know the truth and are *not* doing it right? I've had people say to me, "Our sesshins begin at 3 A.M. When do yours begin? At 4:15? Oh . . . " So this second stage has a lot of arrogance in it. Guilt has a lot of arrogance in it. I'm not saying it's bad to be arrogant; that's just what we are if we don't see.

Yet we make a tremendous effort to be good. I've heard people say, "Well, I was just out of sesshin and someone cut me off on the freeway—and what do you know, I was angry. What a poor student I am . . . " We all do that. See, all wanting—especially wanting to be a certain way—is centered on ego and fear. "If I can be perfect, if I can be realized or enlightened, I will take care of the fear." Do you see the desire there?

There's a tremendous desire to move away from what I am, into an ideal. Some people don't care about enlightenment; but they may feel, "I shouldn't yell at my spouse." Of course you shouldn't yell at your spouse; but the effort to be a person who doesn't yell at your spouse just increases the tension.

To move from being selfish and greedy to trying not to be that way is like taking down all the drab and ugly pictures in your room and putting up pretty pictures. But if that room is a prison cell, you've changed the decorations and they look a little better; but still the freedom you want isn't there; you're still imprisoned in the same room. Changing the pictures on the wall from greed, anger, and ignorance into ideals (that we should not be greedy, angry, or ignorant) improves the decoration, perhaps—but leaves us without freedom.

I'm reminded of an old story about a king who wanted the wisest man among his subjects to be his prime minister. When the search finally was narrowed to three men the king put them to a supreme test: he placed them in a room in his palace and installed an ingenious lock in the door. The candidates were told that the first person to open the door would be appointed prime minister. So two of them started to work out complicated mathematical formulas to discover the proper lock combination. But the third man just sat in his chair for a time—and then, without bothering to put pen to paper, he got up, walked to the door, and turned the knob—and the door opened. It had been unlocked the whole time. What is the point of that story? The prison cell we live in, whose walls we are frantically redecorating, is not a prison cell. In fact the door has never been locked. There is no lock. We don't need to sit in our cells and struggle for freedom by frantically trying to change ourselves—because we are already free.

Merely to say this doesn't solve the problem for us, of course. How can we realize this fact of freedom?

We've said that being selfish and having a desire to be unselfish are both based on fear. Even the desire to be wise, to be perfect, is based on fear. We wouldn't chase the desire if we saw that we were already free. So our practice always comes back to the same thing: how to see more clearly, how not to go down blind alleys, such as that of trying to be unselfish. Instead of going from unconscious selfishness to conscious unselfishness, what we need to do is to see the foolishness of the second stage—or, if we play around in it, at least to be aware that we are doing so. What we need is to go to the *third* stage, which is . . . what?

Initially we must tear the first two stages apart. We do this by becoming the witness. Instead of saying, "I should not be impatient," we observe ourselves being impatient. We stand back and watch. We see the truth of our impatience. The truth is certainly not some mental picture of being nice and patient; in creating that picture we just bury the irritation and anger, which will pop out later. What *is* the truth of any moment of upset, when we are impatient, jealous, or depressed? When we start working like this—which means to really observe our minds—we see that they are constantly spinning dreams of how we should or shouldn't be or how someone else should or shouldn't be; of how we've been in the past, and how we're going to be in the future; of how we can arrange matters to get what we desire.

When we step back and become a patient and persistent witness, we begin to understand that neither of the two stages does ourselves or anyone else any good. Only then can we—without even trying—slip into stage three, which means simply to experience the truth of that moment of impatience, the very fact of just feeling impatient. When we can do that we have slipped out of the duality that says there is me and there is a way I should be—and we return to ourselves as we are. And when we experience ourselves as we are—since the only thing that is holding impatience in place is our thoughts—the impatience begins to resolve itself.

So our practice is about making fear conscious, instead of running around inside our cell of fear, trying to make it look better and feel better. All of our efforts in life are these escaping endeavors: we try to escape the suffering, escape the pain of what we are. Even feeling guilty is an escape. The truth of any moment is always being just as we are. And that means to experience our unkindness when we are unkind. We don't like to do that. We like to think of ourselves as kind people. But often we're not.

When we experience ourselves as we are, then out of that death of the ego, out of that withering, the flower blooms. On a withered tree, the flower blooms—a wonderful line from *Shōyō Rōku*. A flower blooms, not on a decorated tree, but on a withered tree. When we back away from our ideals and investigate them by being the witness, then we back into what we are, which is the intelligence of life itself.

How does the process we're talking about relate to enlightenment? When we back out of unreality by witnessing it, we see it for what it is; we fall into reality. Maybe at first we see it only a second at a time, but over time the percentage goes up. And when we can spend over ninety percent of our time being with life as it is, we're going to see *what* life is. We *are* life, then. When we are anything, we know what it is. We're like the earnest fish that spent its lifetime swimming from teacher to teacher. The fish wanted to know what the ocean was. And some teachers told him, "Well, you have to try very hard to be a good fish. This is a tremendous area that you're investigating. And you have to meditate for long hours, and you have to punish yourself and you have to really try to be a good fish." But the fish at last came to one teacher and asked, "What's the great ocean? What's the great ocean?" And the teacher simply laughed.

WHAT PRACTICE IS

Practice is very simple. That doesn't mean it won't turn our life around, however. I want to review what we do when we sit, or do zazen. And if you think you're beyond this, well, you can think you're beyond this.

Sitting is essentially a simplified space. Our daily life is in constant movement: lots of things going on, lots of people talking, lots of events taking place. In the middle of that, it's very difficult to sense what we are in our life. When we simplify the situation, when we take away the externals and remove ourselves from the ringing phone, the television, the people who visit us, the dog who needs a walk, we get a chance—which is absolutely the most valuable thing there is—to face ourselves. Meditation is not about some state, but about the meditator. It's not about some activity, or about fixing something, or accomplishing something. It's about ourselves. If we don't simplify the situation the chance of taking a good look at ourselves is very small—because what we tend to look at isn't ourselves, but everything else. If something goes wrong, what do we look at? We look at what's going wrong, and usually at others we think have made it go wrong. We're looking *out there* all the time, and not at ourselves.

When I say meditation is about the meditator, I do not mean that we engage in self-analysis. That's not it either. So what *do* we do?

Once we have assumed our best posture (which should be balanced, easy), we just sit there, we do zazen. What do I mean by "just sit there"? It's the most demanding of all activities. Usually in meditation we don't shut our eyes. But right now I'd like you to shut your eyes and just *sit* there. What's going on? All sorts of things. A tiny twitch in your left shoulder; a pressure in your side. . . . Notice your face for a moment. Feel it. Is it tense anywhere? Around the mouth, around the forehead? Now move down a bit. Notice your neck, just feel it. Then your shoulders, your back, chest, abdominal area, your arms, thighs. Keep feeling whatever you find. And feel your breath as it comes and goes. Don't try to control it, just feel it. Our first instinct is to try to control the breath. Just let your breath be as it is. It may be high in your chest, it may be in the middle, it may be low. It may feel tense. Just experience it as it is. Now just feel all of that. If a car goes by outside, hear it. If a plane flies over, notice that. You might hear a refrigerator going on and off. Just be that. That's all you have to do, absolutely all you have to do: experience that, and just stay with it. Now you can open your eyes.

If you can just do that for three minutes, that's miraculous. Usually after about a minute we begin to think. Our interest in just being with reality (which is what we have just done) is very low. "You mean that is all there is to zazen?" We don't like that. "We're seeking enlightenment, aren't we?" Our interest in reality is extremely low. No, we want to think. We want to worry through all of our preoccupations. We want to figure life out. And so before we know it we've forgotten all about this moment, and we've drifted off into thinking about something: our boyfriend, our girlfriend, our child, our boss, our current fear . . . off we go! There's nothing sinful about fantasizing except that when we're lost in that, we've lost something else. When we're lost in thought, when we're dreaming, what have we lost? We've lost reality. Our life has escaped us.

This is what human beings do. And we don't just do it sometimes, we do it most of the time. Why do we do that? You know the answer, of course. We do it because we are trying to protect ourselves. We're trying to rid ourselves of our current difficulty, or at least understand it. There's nothing wrong with our self-centered thoughts except that when we identify with them, our view of reality is blocked. So what should we do when the thoughts come up? We should label the thoughts. Be *specific* in your labeling: not just "thinking, thinking" or "worrying, worrying," but a specific label. For example: "Having a thought she's very bossy." "Having a thought that he's very unfair to me." "Having a thought that I never do anything right." Be specific. And if the thoughts are tumbling out so fast that you can't find anything except confusion, then just label the foggy mess "confusion." But if you persist in trying to find a separate thought, sooner or later you will.

When we practice like this, we get acquainted with ourselves, how our lives work, what we are doing with them. If we find that certain thoughts come up hundreds of times, we know something about ourselves that we didn't know before. Perhaps we incessantly think about the past, or the future. Some people always think about events, some people always think about other people. Some people always think about themselves. Some people's thoughts are almost entirely judgments about other people. Until we have labeled for four or five years, we don't know ourselves very well. When we label thoughts precisely and carefully, what happens to them? They begin to quiet down. We don't have to force ourselves to get rid of them. When they quiet down, we return to the experience of the body and the breath, over and over and over. I can't emphasize enough that we don't just do this three times, we do it ten thousand times; and as we do it, our life transforms. That's a theoretical description of sitting. It's very simple; there's nothing complicated about it.

Now let's take a daily life situation. Suppose you work in an aircraft plant, and you're told that the government contract is coming to an end and probably will not be renewed. You tell yourself, "I'm going to lose my job. I'm going to lose my income. I have a family to support. This is terrible!" What happens then? Your mind starts going over and over and over your problem. "What's going to happen? What shall I do?" Your mind spins faster and faster with worry.

Now there's nothing wrong with planning ahead; we have to plan. But when we become upset, we don't just plan; we obsess. We twist the problem around in a thousand ways. If we don't know what it means to practice with our worried thoughts, what happens next? The thoughts produce an emotion and we become even more agitated. All emotional agitation is caused by the mind. And if we let this happen over a period of time, we often become physically sick or mentally depressed. If the mind will not take care of a situation with awareness, the body will. It will help us out. It's as if the body says, "If you won't take care of it, I guess I've got to." So we produce our next cold, our next rash, our next ulcer, whatever is our style. A mind that is not aware will produce illness. That's not a criticism, however. I don't know of anyone who doesn't get ill, including myself. When the desire to worry is strong, we create difficulties. With regular practice, we just do it less. Anything of which we're unaware will have its fruits in our life, one way or another.

From the human point of view, the things that go wrong in our lives are of two kinds. One kind are events outside of ourselves, and the other are things within us, such as physical illness. Both are our practice, and we handle them in the same way. We label all the thoughts that occur around them, and we experience them in our body. The process is sitting itself.

To talk about this sounds really easy. But to do it is horrendously difficult. I don't know anyone who can do it all of the time. I know of some people who can do it much of the time. But when we practice in this way, becoming aware of everything that enters our life (whether internal or external), our life begins to transform. And we gain strength and insight and even live at times in the enlightened state, which simply means experiencing life as it is. It's not a mystery.

If you are new to practice it's important to realize that simply to sit on that cushion for fifteen minutes is a victory. Just to sit with that much composure, just to be there, is fine.

If we were afraid of being in water and didn't know how to swim, the first victory would be just to lower ourselves into the water. The next step might be getting our face wet. If we were expert swimmers the challenge might be whether we can enter our hand into the water at a certain angle as we execute our stroke. Does that mean that one swimmer is better and the other worse? No. Both of them are perfect for where they are. Practice at any stage is just being who we are at that moment. It's not a question of being good or bad, or better or worse. Sometimes after my talks people will say, "I don't understand that." And that's perfect too. Our understanding grows over the years, but at any point we are perfect in being what we are. Because if we are caught in self-centered emotions we can't see people or situations clearly. A thought in itself is just pure sensory input, an energy fragment. But we fear to see thoughts as they are.

When we label a thought we step back from it, we remove our identification. There's a world of difference between saying, "She's impossible" and "Having a thought that she's impossible." If we persistently label any thought, the emotional overlay begins to drop out and we are left with an impersonal energy fragment to which we need not attach. But if we think our thoughts are real we act out of them. And if we act from such thoughts our life is muddled. Again, practice is to work with this until we know it in our bones. Practice is not about achieving a realization in our heads. It has to be our flesh, our bones, ourself. Of course, we have to have life-centered thoughts: how to follow a recipe, how to put on a roof, how to plan our vacation. But we don't need the emotionally self-centered activity that we call thinking. It really isn't thinking, it's an aberration of thinking.

Zen is about an active life, an involved life. When we know our minds well and the emotions that our thinking creates, we tend to see better what our lives are about and what needs to be done, which is generally just the next task under our nose. Zen is about a life of action, not a life of passively doing nothing. But our actions must be based on reality. When our actions are based on our false thought systems (which are based on our conditioning), they are poorly based. When we have seen through the thought systems we can see what needs to be done.

What we are doing is not reprogramming ourselves, but freeing ourselves from all programs, by seeing that they are empty of reality. Reprogramming is just jumping from one pot into another. We may have what we think of as a better programming; but the point of sitting is not to be run by *any* program. Suppose we have a program called "I lack self-confidence." Suppose we decide to reprogram that to "I have self-confidence." Neither of them will stand up very well under the pressures of life, because they involved an "I." And this "I" is a very fragile creation—unreal, actually—and is easily befuddled. In fact there never was an "I." The point is to see that it is empty, an illusion, which is different from dissolving it. When I say that it's empty, I mean that it has no basic reality; it's just a creation of the self-centered thoughts.

Doing Zen practice is never as simple as talking about it. Even students who have a fair understanding of what they're doing at times tend to desert basic practice. Still, when we sit well, everything else takes care of itself. So whether we have been sitting five years or twenty years or are just beginning, it is important to sit with great, meticulous care.

TWO

STEM

WHIRLPOOLS AND STAGNANT
WATERS

We are like whirlpools in the river of life. In flowing forward, a river or stream may hit rocks, branches, or irregularities in the ground, causing whirlpools to spring up spontaneously here and there. Water entering one whirlpool quickly passes through and rejoins the river, eventually joining another whirlpool and moving on. Though for short periods it seems to be distinguishable as a separate event, the water in the whirlpools is just the river itself. The stability of a whirlpool is only temporary. The energy of the river of life forms living things—a human being, a cat or dog, trees and plants—then what held the whirlpool in place is itself altered, and the whirlpool is swept away, reentering the larger flow. The energy that was a particular whirlpool fades out and the water passes on, perhaps to be caught again and turned for a moment into another whirlpool.

We'd rather not think of our lives in this way, however. We don't want to see ourselves as simply a temporary formation, a whirlpool in the river of life. The fact is, we take form for a while; then when conditions are appropriate, we fade out. There's nothing wrong with fading out; it's a natural part of the process. However, we want to think that this little whirlpool that we are isn't part of the stream. We want to see ourselves as permanent and stable. Our whole energy goes into trying to protect our supposed separateness. To protect the separateness, we set up artificial, fixed boundaries; as a consequence, we accumulate excess baggage, stuff that slips into our whirlpool and can't flow out again. So things clog up our whirlpool and the process gets messy. The stream needs to flow naturally and freely. If our particular whirlpool is all bogged down, we also impair the energy of the stream itself. It can't go anywhere. Neighboring whirlpools may get less water because of our frantic holding on. What we can best do for ourselves and for life is to keep the water in our whirlpool rushing and clear so that it is just flowing in and flowing out. When it gets all clogged up, we create troubles— mental, physical, spiritual.

We serve other whirlpools best if the water that enters ours is free to rush through and move on easily and quickly to whatever else needs to be stirred. The energy of life seeks rapid transformation. If we can see life this way and not cling to anything, life simply comes and goes. When debris flows into our little whirlpool, if the flow is even and strong, the debris rushes around for a while and then goes on its way. Yet that's not how we live our lives. Not seeing that we are simply a whirlpool in the river of the universe, we view ourselves as separate entities, needing to protect our boundaries. The very judgment "I feel hurt" establishes a boundary, by naming an "I" that demands to be protected. Whenever trash floats into our whirlpool, we make great efforts to avoid it, to expel it, or to somehow control it.

Ninety percent of a typical human life is spent trying to put boundaries around the whirlpool. We're constantly on guard: "He might hurt me." "This might go wrong." "I don't like him anyway." This is a complete misuse of our life function; yet we all do it to some degree.

Financial worries reflect our struggle to maintain fixed boundaries. "What if my investment doesn't work out? I might lose all of my money." We don't want anything to threaten our money supply. We all think that would be a terrible thing. By being protective and anxious, clinging to our assets, we clog up our lives. Water that should be rushing in and out, so it can serve, becomes stagnant. A whirlpool that puts up a dam around itself and shuts itself off from the river becomes stagnant and loses its vitality. Practice is about no longer being caught in the particular, and instead seeing it for what it is—a part of the whole. Yet we spend most of our energies creating stagnant water. That's what living in fear will do. The fear exists because the whirlpool doesn't understand what it is—none other than the stream itself. Until we get an inkling of that truth, all of our energies go in the wrong direction. We create many stagnant pools, which breed contamination and disease. Pools seeking to dam themselves for protection begin to contend with one another. "You're smelly. I don't like you." Stagnant pools cause a lot of trouble. The freshness of life is gone.

Zen practice helps us to see how we have created stagnation in our lives. "Have I always been so angry, and just never noticed it?" So our first discovery in practice is to recognize our own stagnation, created by our self-centered thoughts. The biggest problems are created by attitudes we cannot see in ourselves. Unacknowledged depression, fear, and anger create rigidity. When we recognize the rigidity and stagnation, the water begins to flow again, bit by bit. So the most vital part of practice is to be willing to be life itself—which is simply the incoming sensations—that which creates our whirlpool.

Over the years, we have trained ourselves to do the opposite: to create stagnant pools. This is our false accomplishment. Out of this ongoing effort come all of our troubles and our separation from life. We don't know how to be intimate, to be the stream of life. A stagnant whirlpool with defended boundaries isn't close to anything. Caught in a self-centered dream, we suffer, as one of our daily Zen Center vows states. Practice is the slow reversal of that. With most students, this reversal is the work of a lifetime. The change is often painful, especially at first. When we are used to the rigidity and controlled stiffness of a defended life, we don't want to allow fresh currents into awareness, however refreshing they may truly be.

The truth is, we don't like fresh air very much. We don't like fresh water very much. It takes a long time before we can see our defensiveness and manipulation of life in our daily activities. Practice helps us to see these maneuvers more clearly, and such recognition is always unpleasant. Still, it's essential that we see what we are doing. The longer we practice, the more readily we can recognize our defensive patterns. The process is never easy or painless, however, and those who are hoping to find a quick and easy place of rest should not undertake it.

What we do get out of practice is being more awake. Being more alive. Knowing our own mischievous tendencies so well that we don't need to visit them on others. We learn that it's never okay to yell at somebody just because we feel upset. Practice helps us to realize where our life is stagnant. Unlike rushing mountain streams, with wonderful water flowing in and flowing out, we may be brought to a dead halt by "I don't like it. . . . He really hurt my feelings," or "I have such a hard life." In truth, there is only the ongoing rush of the water. What we call our life is nothing but a little detour, a whirlpool that springs up, then fades away. Sometimes the detours are tiny and very brief: life swirls for a year or two in one place, then is wiped away. People wonder why some babies die when they are young. Who knows? We don't know why. It is part of this endless rushing of energy. When we can join this, we're at peace. When all of our efforts go in the opposite direction, we are not at peace.

EXPERIENCES AND EXPERIENCING

At each second, we are at a crossroad: between unawareness and awareness, between being absent and being present—or between experiences and experiencing. Practice is about moving from experiences to experiencing. What is meant by this?

We tend to overwork the word *experience,* and when we say, "Be with your experience," we are speaking carelessly. It may not be helpful to follow this advice. Ordinarily we see our lives as series of experiences. For example, I have an experience of one or another person, an experience of my lunch or my office. From this point of view, my life is nothing but having one experience after another. Entwined around each experience there may be a slight halo or a neurotic emotional veil. Often the veil takes the form of memories, fantasies, or hopes for the future—the associations we bring to experience, as a result of our past conditioning. When we do zazen, our experience may be dominated by our memories, which can be overwhelming.

Is there anything wrong with this? Humans *do* have memories, fantasies, hopes; that's natural. When we clothe our experience with these associations, however, experience becomes an object: a noun rather than a verb. So our lives become encounters with one object after another: persons, my lunch, my office. Memories and hopes are similar: life becomes a series of "this" and "that." We ordinarily see our lives as encounters with things "out there." Life becomes dualistic: subject and object, me and that.

There's no problem with this process—unless we believe it. For when we really believe that we're meeting objects all day long, we're enslaved. Why? Because any object "out there" will have a slight veil of emotional context. And we then react in terms of our emotional associations. In classical Zen teaching, we are enslaved by greed, anger, and ignorance. To see the world exclusively in this way is to be in chains. When our world consists of objects, we guide our lives by what we can expect from each object: "Does he like me?" "Is that to my advantage?" "Should I be afraid of her?" Our history and our memories take over, and we divide the world up into things to avoid and things to pursue.

The trouble with this way of living is that what benefits me now may hurt me later, and vice versa. The world is constantly changing, and so our associations lead us astray. There's nothing safe about a world of objects. We're constantly wary, even of those people whom we say we love and are close to. As long as another person is an object to us, we can be sure that there's no genuine love or compassion between us.

If having experiences is our ordinary world, what is the other world, the other fork in the road? What is the difference between experiences and experiencing? What is genuine hearing, touching, tasting, seeing, and so on?

When experiencing occurs, in that very moment, experiencing is not in space or time. It can't be; for when it's in space or time, we've made an object of it.

As we touch and look and hear, we're creating the world of space and time, but the actual life we lead is not in space or time; it's just experiencing. The world of space and time arises when experiencing becomes reduced to a series of experiences. In the precise moment of hearing, for example, there is just hearing, hearing, hearing, hearing, which creates the sound of the airplane or whatever. Thup, thup, thup, thup . . . : there's space between each; and each one is absolute hearing, hearing, hearing. That's our life, as we create our world. We're creating with all our senses so quickly that we can't possibly keep track of it. The world of our experiences is being created out of nothing, second by second by second.

In the service we do, one of the dedications states, "Unceasing change turns the wheel of life." Experiencing, experiencing, experiencing; change, change, change. "Unceasing change turns the wheel of life, and so reality is shown in all its many forms. Peaceful dwelling as change itself liberates all suffering sentient beings and brings them to great joy." Peaceful dwelling as change itself means feeling the throbbing pain in my legs, hearing the sound of a car: just experiencing, experiencing. Just dwelling with experience itself. Even the pain is changing minutely, second by second by second. "Peaceful dwelling as change itself liberates all suffering sentient beings and brings them to great joy."

If this process were absolutely clear, we'd have no need to practice. The enlightened state is not *having* an experience; instead, it's an absence of all experience. The enlightened state is pure, unadulterated experiencing. And that is utterly different from "having an enlightenment experience." Enlightenment is the demolition of all experience built of thoughts, fantasies, memories, and hopes. Frankly, we're not interested in demolishing our lives as we have ordinarily known them. We demolish the false structures of our lives by labeling our thoughts, by saying for the five hundredth time, "Having a thought that such-and-such will happen." When we've said it five hundred times, we see it for what it is. It's just empty energy spinning out of our conditioning, with no reality whatsoever. There is no intrinsic truth in it; it's just changing, changing, changing.

It's easy for us to talk about this process, but there's nothing that we are less interested in doing than demolishing our fantasy structures. We have a secret fear that if we demolished them all, we'd be demolishing ourselves.

There's an old Sufi story about a man who dropped his keys on the dark side of the street at night, then crossed the street to the lamppost where it was bright to look for the keys. When a friend asked why he was looking under the lamp instead of where he dropped the keys, he replied, "I'm looking here because there is more light." That's what we do with our lives: the familiar framework is where we want to look. If we have a problem, we follow a familiar framework: thinking, stewing, analyzing, keeping the crazy business of our lives going because that's what we're used to doing. Never mind that it doesn't work. We just get more determined, and keep searching under the lamppost. We're not interested in that life which is out of space and time, constantly creating the world of space and time. We're not interested in that; in fact, it's frightening to us.

What pushes us to abandon this melodrama, to sit through the confusion? At bottom, it comes down to the unease we have with the way we are living our lives. Beyond a life of having experiences is a life of experiencing, a life of compassion and joy. For true compassion and joy are not things to be experienced. Our true master is just this: changing, changing, changing; experiencing, experiencing, experiencing. The master is not in space and time—yet none other than space and time. Our experiencing of life is also the creating of life itself. "Unceasing change turns the wheel of life and so reality is shown in all its many forms."

A poem by W. H. Auden captures much of our ordinary state:

> We would rather be ruined than changed,
> We would rather die in our dread
> Than climb the cross of the moment
> And let our illusions die.

We would rather be ruined than changed—even though change is who we are. We would rather die in our anxiety, our fear, our loneliness, than climb the cross of the moment and let our illusions die. And the cross is also the crossroads, the choice. We are here to make that choice.

PRACTICING WITH RELATIONSHIPS

The mind of the past is ungraspable;
the mind of the future is ungraspable;
the mind of the present is ungraspable.

DIAMOND SUTRA

What is time? Is there time? What can we say about our daily life in connection with time, and with no-time, no-self? What can we learn about relationships in connection with this no-time, no-self?

Ordinarily we think of a dharma talk or a concert or any event in life as having a beginning, a middle, and an end. But at any point in this talk, for instance, if I stop right now, where are the words I've already said? They just don't exist. If I stop at any later point in the talk, where are the words that have been said up to that point? They don't exist. And when the talk's over, where is the talk? There is no talk. All that's left are memory traces in our brains. And this memory, whatever it is, is fragmentary and incomplete; we remember only parts of any actual experience. The same thing could be said for a concert—in fact we can say the same thing about our whole day, and our whole life. At this very point in time, where is our past life? It doesn't exist.

Now, how does this pertain to relationships, to our relationships with anything and anyone—to our relationship to our sitting cushion, to our breakfast, to a person, to the office, to our children?

The way we usually hold a relationship is that, "This relationship is there, *out* there, and it's supposed to give *me* pleasure. At the very least, it shouldn't give me discomfort." In other words we make this relationship into a dish of ice cream. That dish of ice cream is there to give me pleasure and give me comfort. And very few of us view our relationship in any other light than, "There it is; I've picked you out, and you know what you're supposed to do." So ordinarily when we worry about relationships, we're not talking about the nice parts. Often the nice parts may even be predominant. But what we're interested in is the *unpleasantness:* "It shouldn't be there." And when I say "unpleasant," it could range from just annoyance to a state more intense than that.

So how is all this related to no-time, no-self?

Let's take a quarrel at breakfast. At lunchtime we're still upset; not only upset but we're telling everybody about it, getting comfort, sympathy, agreement—and already we're in our heads. "When I see him tonight we'll really have to discuss it; we'll have to really get at this matter." So there's the breakfast quarrel, there's the luncheon upset, and then there's the future—what we're going to do about the upset.

But what's really *here?* What's really *now?* As we sit having our lunch, where is that breakfast quarrel? Where is it? "The mind of the past is ungraspable."

Where *is* it? The dinner, when we're going to really fix all this up (to our satisfaction, of course), where *is* it? "The mind of the future is ungraspable." It doesn't exist.

What *does* exist? What's real? There is just my upset right now, at lunch. My story describing what happened at breakfast is not what happened. It's *my story*. What is real is the headache, the fluttering in my tummy. And my chattering is a manifestation of that physical energy. Outside of the physical experience, there is nothing else that's real. And I don't know if *that's* real, but that's all we can say about it.

A few weeks ago a young woman (not a student of Zen) came to talk to me and wanted to tell me about what her husband did to her three weeks before. She was very, very upset; she could hardly speak she was so upset. So I said, "Where is your husband right now?" "Oh, my husband's at work." "Well, where is the upset, where is this quarrel, where is it?" "Well,

I'm telling you about it." I said, "But where is it? Show it to me." "Well I can't show it to you, but I'm telling you about it. See, this is the way it was." "But when was it?" "Three weeks ago." "Where is it?" "Oh . . . " She was getting more and more annoyed. Finally she could see that none of the upset had any reality whatsoever. And then she said, "But if that's all there is, how can I fix up my husband?"

Now the point is that we build up elaborate systems, emotions, and drama out of our belief in time — past, present, and future. Every one of us has done this. And believe me, doing this is no trivial thing. People have put themselves—and I've done it too—into such a state they can hardly function; they can't take care of their obligations, and they make themselves sick, physically and mentally.

Now, does this mean that we do nothing if we're upset? No, we do what we do. Definitely we just do what we do and at every point we are doing the best we can.

But action based on confusion and ignorance leads directly to more confusion, upset, and ignorance. It's not good or bad, and we all do it without exception. So in our ignorance, in our belief in this linear life—"That happened yesterday," and "Here it is and it's going to go on and on and on"—we live in a world of complaints, as a victim or an aggressor, in what seems to be a hostile world.

Now just one thing and one thing alone creates this hostile world, and that is our thoughts—our pictures and our fantasies. They create a world of time and space and suffering. And yet, if we try to find the past and the future that our thoughts dwell upon, we find it is impossible—they are ungraspable.

One student told me he had been climbing a wall since he heard me talk about time, because he's been looking for his past. He said, "If there is no past and no future and I can't even get hold of the present—I mean I try to get hold of it, and it's gone—then who am I?" A good question; one that we can all ask. "Who am I?"

Let's take a typical thought, the sort we all have: "Bill makes me sick." Already there is me and Bill and this feeling sick, this emotion. There's me and Bill and the sickness. Everything is all spread out. Right now I've created me, I've created Bill, and somehow out of all that, there's this upset.

Now let's say it instead: "Me/Bill/sick." All one. "MeBillsick." Just the experience, as it is, right now. And always we'll find that if we just are the experience, the solution is contained in it. And not even just contained in it; the experience *itself* and the solution are not two separate things. But the minute we say, "She made me sick." "He annoys me." "We did this." "She did that." "It makes me sick; makes me annoyed;

really hurts my feelings," then we have you, the other person, and whatever you're cooking up about it. Instead of: there's nothing—except this very present ungraspable moment of meyouanger. Just being that, right there the solution is obvious.

But as long as we spin our thoughts, such as, "Bill makes me sick," we have a problem. You'll notice that the sentence has a beginning, a middle, and an end; and out of that comes this world: hostile, frightening, and separate.

See, there is nothing wrong with our sentences. And we all have to live in a relative world; it looks like breakfast, lunch, and dinner. And there's nothing wrong with the conceptual relative world. What goes "wrong" is that we don't see it for what it is. And not seeing it for what it is, we tend to pick our friends and lovers much as we turn on the TV.

For instance, we meet a nice girl and, "Hm, she looks like Channel 4 and I'm always calm and comfortable with Channel 4; I know what to expect on Channel 4; a certain range of this and that; a little news—I can be pretty comfortable with a Channel 4 person." So we get together and for a while everything goes very well. There is a lot of comfort and agreement. It seems like a great relationship.

But lo and behold, what happens after a while? Somehow Channel 4 has switched over to Channel 63, a lot of irritation and anger; sometimes Channel 49, all dreams and fantasies. And what am I doing during all this? See, I was pretending to be just a Channel 4 person. But no, it seems I like to spend a lot of time at Channel 33 with childhood cartoons, mostly about my dream prince or princess. And then I have other channels like Channel 19—gloom, depression, and withdrawal. And sometimes, just when I'm into gloom, depression and withdrawal, she's into fantasy and light; that doesn't fit very well. Or sometimes all the channels seem to play at once. We have upset and a lot of noise, and one or both of the partners fights or withdraws.

What to do? We are now into our usual mess, our usual scenario; and we have to try to fix it, don't we? Somehow, all was happy once. So what we've got to do, *obviously,* is to make both of us get back on Channel 4. And we say to her, "You should be like this; you should do that: that's the person I fell in love with." For a while both parties make an effort, because there is an artificial peace on Channel 4 (and a lot of boredom). Actually most marriages look like this after a time. Somebody said you can tell who in a restaurant is married—it's the couple who don't talk to each other.

It's interesting that the question nobody asks as the channels become confused is, "*Who* turned the channels on? *Who* is the *source* of all this activity?" In a way there is nothing wrong with the channels. But we never ask who turned the channels on. Who turned our acts on? What's the source? This is the key question to ask.

If we don't ask this question, and the suffering gets bad enough, sometimes we just leave the relationship and look for a new Channel 4—because if we like Channel 4s we tend to keep picking them. And this whole scenario is true not only for intimate relationships, but at the office, on a vacation, or anywhere. This is what we do.

After a number of these unfortunate episodes, we may begin to look at the whole picture of our life. Once in a while, a rare, lucky individual really begins to examine this whole question of what he's doing with his life, and begins to ask the basic questions, "Who am I? Where did I come from? Where will I go?"

Sometimes, very sadly, we may realize that after living with someone for a long time, we have never met him, have never known him. I did this for fifteen years. Some people live out a lifetime and never meet.

Their channels meet once in a while, but *they* never meet.

Then we may be fortunate and encounter a great teaching. And in the Buddhist tradition the Buddha's teaching says, "*It* completely clears all pain. This is the truth, not a lie." We may not have any idea what this means; but, if we are among the lucky ones, we may begin an intelligent practice in an effort to understand the teaching.

Intelligent zazen means making a subtle shift *constantly,* step by step; first from the grosser levels to the more subtle, and to the more subtle, and to the more subtle; beginning to see right through what we call our personality, this one that we've been talking about. We begin to really look at the mind, the body, the thoughts, the sense perceptions, everything that we thought was ourself.

The first part of our practice is as if we were in the middle of a confused, busy street; we can hardly find an empty place and the traffic is going every which way. It's confusing and frightening. And that's the way our life feels to most of us. We're so busy jumping out of the way of what's coming toward us that we can't understand our own entrapment in the traffic. But if we watch it for a while we begin to see that there are holes in the traffic here and there. We might even step up on the sidewalk and begin to take a more objective look. And no matter how busy the traffic, here and there, we begin to notice clear areas.

Now our third step might be to go into a tall building and climb up onto the third-floor balcony and observe the traffic from there. Now it looks different; we can see the direction of it, which way it's moving. We see that in a way it doesn't have anything to do with us, it's just going on.

If we climb higher and higher and higher, eventually we see that the traffic is just patterns; it's beautiful, not frightening. It's just what it is and we begin to see it as a tremendous panorama. We begin to see areas of difficulty as part of the whole, not necessarily good or bad; just part of life. And after years of practice we may reach a place where we just enjoy what we see; enjoy ourselves, enjoy everything just as it is. We can enjoy it but not be caught by it, seeing its impermanence, its flow.

Then we go further, to the stage of being the witness of our life. It's all going on, it's all enjoyable; we're not caught by any of it. And in the final state of our practice we're back in the street, back in the marketplace, right in the middle of the hubbub. But seeing the confusion for what it is, we're free of it. We can love it, enjoy it, serve it, and our life is seen as what it always has been—free and liberated.

Now the first place, where we're caught right in the middle of the traffic and the confusion, is where many of us start our practice. That's where many of us see our relationships as being confusion, puzzlement, and bitterness, because we expect our relationship to be the *one* place that gives us peace from the traffic.

However, as we endeavor to practice with relationships, we begin to see that they are our best way to grow. In them we can see what our mind, our body, our senses, and our thoughts really are. Why are relationships such excellent practice? Why do they help us to go into what we might call the slow death of the ego? Because, aside from our formal sitting, there is no way that is superior to relationships in helping us see where we're stuck and what we're holding on to. As long as our buttons are pushed, we have a great chance to learn and grow. So a relationship is a great gift, not because it makes us happy—it often doesn't— but because any intimate relationship, if we view it as practice, is the clearest mirror we can find.

You might say that relationships are the open door to our true self, to no-self. In our fear we always keep knocking at a painted door, one made of our dreams, our hopes, our ambitions; and we avoid the pain of the gateless gate, the open door of being with what is, whatever it is, here and now.

It's interesting to me that people don't see any connection between their misery and their complaints—their feeling of being a victim; the feeling that everyone is doing something *to* them. It's amazing. How many times has this connection been pointed out in dharma talks? How many? And yet because of our fear we won't look.

Only people of intelligence, energy, and patience will find that still point on which the universe turns. And unfortunately, life for those who cannot or will not face this present moment is often violent and punishing; it's not nice; it doesn't care. Still, the truth is that it's not life, it's ourselves who are creating this misery. But if we really refuse to look at what we are doing—and I'm sorry how few people will look—then we're going to be punished by our life. And then we wonder why it's so hard on us. However, for those who patiently practice—sitting, sitting, sitting; who begin to practice steadily in their daily life—for those people there will be more and more a taste of the joy in a relationship in which no-self meets no-self. In other words openness meets openness. It's very rare, but it does happen. And when it happens I don't even know if we can use the word "relationship." Who is there to relate to whom? You can't say no-self relates to no-self. So for this state there are no words. And in this timeless love and compassion there is, as the Third Patriarch said, "No yesterday, no tomorrow, and no today."

THREE

FLOWER

SIMPLE MIND

The only mind that can sense life in a transformed way is a simple mind. The dictionary defines *simple* as "having or composed of one part only." Awareness can take in a multiplicity of things, just as an eye can take in many details at once. But awareness itself is one thing only. It remains unchanged, without additions or modifications. Awareness is completely simple; we don't have to add anything to it or change it. It is unassuming or unpretentious; it can't help but be that way. Awareness is not a thing, to be affected by this or that. When we live from pure awareness, we are not affected by our past, our present, or our future. Because awareness has nothing it can pretend to, it's humble. It is lowly. Simple.

Practice is about developing or uncovering a simple mind. For example, I often hear people complain that they feel overwhelmed by their lives. To be overwhelmed is to be caught by all the objects, the thoughts, the events of life, and to be affected emotionally by them, so that we feel angry and upset. When we feel like that, we may do and say things that hurt ourselves or other people. Unlike the simple mind of pure awareness, we are confused by the multiplicity of the external environment. Then we can't see that everything external is us. We can't see that everything exists in us until we can live eighty or ninety percent out of a simple mind. Practice is about developing this kind of mind. It is not easy. It takes endless patience, diligence, and determination.

Within this simplicity, this awareness, we understand past, present, and future, and we begin to be less affected by the barrage of experiences. We can live our life with appreciation and some compassion. No longer does our life revolve around judgments, such as: "Oh, he's so hard on me. I'm such a victim." "You hurt my feelings." "You're not the way I want you to be."

People sometimes tell me that after sesshin, life just flows, without any problem. The same issues are there, but they present less difficulty. That happens because in sesshin, mind becomes more simple. Unfortunately, we tend to lose this simplicity, because we again become caught in what appears to be a very complex life around us. We feel that things aren't the way we want them to be, and we begin to struggle and to be at the mercy of our emotions. When this happens, we often behave in destructive ways.

The longer we sit, the more we have periods—at first brief, then longer—when we sense that we don't need to be opposed to others, even when they are difficult. Instead of seeing them as problems, we begin to enjoy their foibles, without having to fix them. For example, we can enjoy the fact that they're too silent, or they talk too much, or they put on too much makeup. To enjoy the world without judgment is what a realized life is like. It takes years and years and years of practice. Even then, I don't mean that every problem can be experienced without reaction; still, a shift occurs, and we move away from a purely reactive life, in which everything that happens can trigger our favorite defense.

A simple mind is not mysterious. In a simple mind, awareness just is. It's open, transparent. There's nothing complicated about it. For most of us most of the time, however, it is largely unavailable. But the more we have contact with a simple mind, the more we sense that everything is ourselves, and the more we feel responsibility for everything. When we sense our connectedness, we have to act differently.

When we get caught in our own thinking, we're not doing our work—feeling the past and the future, all in the present. We even imagine that if we're isolated in a room by ourselves, just being upset, it's okay. The truth is, however, that when we indulge ourselves in this way, we're not doing our work, and the whole of our life is affected. When we maintain awareness, whether we know it or not, healing is taking place. If we practice long enough we begin to sense the truth: we come to understand that the "now" embraces the past and future and the present. When we can sit with a simple mind, not being caught by our own thoughts, something slowly dawns, and a door that has been shut begins to open. For that to occur, we have to work with our anger, our upset, our judgments, our self-pity, our ideas that the past determines the present. As the door opens, we see that the present is absolute and that, in a sense, the whole universe begins right now, in each second. And the healing of life is in that second of simple awareness.

Healing is always just being here, with a simple mind.

JOY

I'm often accused of emphasizing the difficulties in practice. The accusation is true. Believe me, the difficulties are there. If we don't recognize them and why they arise, we tend to fool ourselves. Still, the ultimate reality—not only in our sitting, but also in our lives—is joy. By joy I don't mean happiness; they're not the same. Happiness has an opposite; joy does not. As long as we seek happiness, we're going to have unhappiness, because we always swing from one pole to the other.

From time to time, we do experience joy. It can arise accidentally or in the course of our sitting or elsewhere in our lives. For a while after sesshin, we may experience joy. Over years of practice, our experience of joy deepens—if, that is, we understand practice and are willing to do it. Most people are not.

Joy isn't something we have to find. Joy is who we

are if we're not preoccupied with something else. When we try to find joy, we are simply adding a thought—and an unhelpful one, at that—onto the basic fact of what we are. We don't need to go looking for joy. But we do need to do something. The question is, what? Our lives don't feel joyful, and we keep trying to find a remedy.

Our lives are basically about perception. By perception I mean whatever the senses bring in. We see, we hear, we touch, we smell, and so on. That's what life really is. Most of the time, however, we substitute another activity for perception; we cover it over with something else, which I'll call evaluation. By evaluation, I don't mean an objective, dispassionate analysis—as for example when we look over a messy room and consider or evaluate how to clean it up. The evaluation I have in mind is ego centered: "Is this next episode in my life going to bring me something I like, or not? Is it going to hurt, or isn't it? Is it pleasant or unpleasant? Does it make me important or unimportant? Does it give me something material?" It's our nature to evaluate in this way. To the extent that we give ourselves over to evaluation of this kind, joy will be missing from our lives.

It's amazing how quickly we can switch into evaluation. Perhaps we're functioning pretty well—and then suddenly somebody criticizes what we're doing. In a fraction of a second, we jump into our thoughts. We're quite willing to get into that interesting space of judging others or ourselves. There's a lot of drama in all of this, and we like it, more than we realize. Unless the drama becomes lengthy and punishing, we enter willingly into it, because as human beings we have a basic orientation toward drama. From an ordinary point of view, to be in a world of pure perception is pretty dull.

Suppose we've been away on vacation for a week, and we come back. Perhaps we've enjoyed ourselves, or we think we have. When we return to work, the "In" box is loaded with things to do, and scattered all over the desk are little messages, "While You Were Out." When people call us at work, it usually means that they want something. Perhaps the job we left for someone else to take care of has been neglected. Immediately, we're evaluating the situation. "Who fouled up?" "Who slacked off?" "Why is she calling? I bet it's the same old problem." "It's their responsibility anyway. Why are they calling me?" Likewise, at the end of sesshin we may experience the flow of a joyful life; then we wonder where it goes. Though it doesn't go anywhere, something has happened: a cloud covers the clarity.

Until we know that joy is exactly what's happening, minus our opinion of it, we're going to have only a small amount of joy. When we stay with perception rather than getting lost in evaluation, however, joy can be the person who didn't do the job while we were gone. It can be the interesting encounter on the phone with all of the people we have to call, no matter what they want. Joy can be having a sore throat; it can be getting laid off; it can be unexpectedly having to work overtime. It can be having to take a math exam or dealing with one's former spouse who wants more money. Usually we don't think that these things are joy.

Practice is about dealing with suffering. It's not that the suffering is important or valuable in itself, but that suffering is our teacher. It's the other side of life, and until we can see all of life, there's not going to be any joy. To be honest, sesshin is controlled suffering. We get a chance to face our suffering in a practice situation. As we sit, all the traditional attributes of a good Zen student come under fire: endurance, humility, patience, compassion. These things sound great in books, but they're not so attractive when we're hurting. That's why sesshin ought not to be easy: we need to learn to be with our suffering and still act appropriately. When we learn to be with our experience, whatever it is, we are more aware of the joy that is our life. Sesshin is a good chance to learn this lesson. When we're prepared to practice, suffering can be a fortunate thing. None of us wants to recognize this fact. I certainly try to avoid suffering; there are lots of things I don't want happening in my life. Still, if we can't learn to be our experience even when it hurts, we'll never know joy. Joy is being the circumstances of our life just as they are. If someone's been unfair to us, that's it. If someone's telling lies about us, that's it also.

The material wealth of this country in some ways makes it more difficult for us to experience the basic joy that we are. Travelers to India sometimes report that along with the enormous poverty, there is an extraordinary joy. Faced with life and death all the time, the people have learned something that is hard for most of us: they have learned to appreciate each moment. We don't do very well with that. Our very prosperity—all of the things we take for granted and all of the things we want more of—is in a way a barrier. There are other barriers, more basic ones. But our wealth is certainly part of the problem.

In practice, we return over and over again to perception, to just sitting. Practice is just hearing, just seeing, just feeling. This is what Christians call the face of God: simply taking in this world as it manifests. We feel our body; we hear the cars and birds. That's all there is. But we are unwilling to stay in that space for more than a few seconds. We go shooting off, remembering what happened to us last week or thinking about what's going to happen next week. We obsess about persons that we're having trouble with or about our work or whatever. There's nothing wrong with these ideas popping up, but if we get stuck in them, we're into the world of evaluation from our self-centered viewpoint. Most of us spend most of our lives in this viewpoint.

It's natural to think, "If I didn't have such a difficult partner (or difficult roommate or difficult something else), then I know my life would be much calmer. I would be much better able to appreciate my life." That might be true for a short time. Life would feel better for a time, of course. But such comfort is not as valuable as facing what upsets us, because it's this very upset (our tendency to get attached to our dramas, to get involved in them and get our mind racing and our emotions fired up) that is the barrier. There is no real joy in such a life, no joy at all. So we run from difficulties; we try to eliminate something—our partner, our roommate, our whatever—so that we can find a perfect place where nothing can upset us. Does anybody have a place like that? Where could it be? What could even approximate it? Years ago I used to allow myself ten minutes a day to daydream about a tropical island, and every day I would furnish my little hut. My fantasy life got better and better. Finally, I had all of the conveniences. Wonderful food just showed up, and there was the gentle ocean and a lagoon, just right for swimming, next to the hut. It's fine to daydream consciously if there is a time limit. But my dream couldn't exist, except in my mind. There is no place on earth where we can be free of ourselves. If we were sitting in a cave meditating, we'd still be thinking about something: "How noble of me it is to sit in this cave!" And after a while: "What excuse can I invent to get out of here and not look bad?" If we stop ourselves and find out what we're really feeling or thinking, we'll notice—even if we're working hard—a thin veil of self-concern over our activity. Enlightenment is simply not doing this. Enlightenment is simply doing what we're doing totally, responding to things as they come up. The modern term is "being in the flow." Joy is just this: something comes up; I perceive it. Something is needed, and I do it, and then the next thing, and the next. I take some time out for a walk or to talk to my friends. There is no problem in a life lived in this way.

NOTES

WHIRLPOOLS AND STAGNANT WATERS

p. 39 **Caught in a self-centered dream** The vows are as follows: "Caught in a self-centered dream: only suffering. / Holding to self-centered thoughts: exactly the dream. / Each moment, life as it is: the only teacher. / Being just this moment: compassion's way."

EXPERIENCES AND EXPERIENCING

p. 49 **We would rather be ruined** W. H. Auden, from "The Age of Anxiety," in *Collected Poems,* ed. by Edward Mendelson (New York: Random House, 1976), p. 407.

RHEA FELLERS LOUDEN

CHARLOTTE JOKO BECK is the author of the bestselling *Everyday Zen* and *Nothing Special*. She teaches at the San Diego Zen Center.

🍃